To Laura —

Run Fast Friend.

What People Are Saying About *Runner's Fix* . . .

"Mike is one of the best out there. We trust his judgement and expertise with running injuries, without hesitation. Over the years, we have sent countless athletes his way and referred runners from other area schools to him, based on his reputation for not just looking for a 'quick fix' that will get the athlete healthy for the short term, but rather solve the root of the issue at hand. It is rare to find a PT that truly appreciates and understands runners and their injuries. His expertise from years of firsthand experience with runners of all ages keeps us coming back to him time and time again."

—Asa Kelly, Benzie Central Boys & Girls
Cross-Country and Track & Field Coach
10x State Champion Coach
10x State Runner Up Coach
8x State Coach of the Year
20x State Coach of the Year Nominee
3x National Coach of the Year Nominee
5x Individual State Champion Coach

"Mike Swinger's book is a 'must-have guide' for those dealing with an injury or pain, whether they are an athlete, coach or weekend warrior. Mike's practical, well-thought-out and easy-read guide makes sense and as a coach of runners, a retired physical educator, and an active person myself, he has helped me and my athletes come back from injuries as well as teaching us about *why* it happened and the way to recovery. I wished I would have had this book a long time ago. Keep it handy, you'll be glad you did."

—John Lober, Traverse City Central Boys Track & Field Coach
2014 NFHS "National High School Track Coach of the Year"
2015 NHSACA "National High School Track Coach of the Year"
2006 Inducted into the MITCA Hall of Fame

"Mike Swinger has taken his expertise as a physical therapist and 'opened the door' for both the novice and advanced runner to run with ease and comfort. This book allows one to go to the section corresponding to the body parts that are hurting and work through the appropriate stretches and/or strengthening exercises that will benefit. All suggested movements are demonstrated via his website runphys.com/injuryprevention. A 'must have' for any runner!"

—Martin J. Faasse, D.P.M., Grandville, MI

"I am so excited that Mike Swinger has written this book! I love having this information in hand to refer to in order to prevent injury. That is, once Mike has gotten me healthy in the first place.

"I have been seeing Mike as my physical therapist for a few years and can't say enough about his ability as a diagnostician and also as a hands-on healer. From his assessment to his hands-on treatment to his plan for prevention of future injury, Mike's skill is unmatched. He understands the runner's body and mentality, and uses his complete understanding of the body's mechanics to get you better and keep you running healthy as long as you want to continue running.

"Time and time again, Mike has impressed me with his ability to diagnose, treat, and prevent—and that is testimony to his superior expertise in his field. I trust Mike Swinger with my body, as well as my friends' and family's bodies and also refer patients to him regularly. As a physician, it is comforting to be able to send patients to a therapist I have full confidence in. Now that you have this book, you can keep Mike Swinger's expert insight and knowledge base with you 24/7/365. Refer to it often and use this information to stay healthy. Godspeed!"

—Dr. Jacob Flynn, M.D.
NCAA Division 1 All-American Central Michigan University
Mr. Cross-Country State of Michigan
3x High School Cross-Country State Champion
PRs: Mile 4:08, 5K 14:10, 10K 29:10

"Mike is a phenomenal physical therapist who I have been lucky enough to know for the past decade. He truly is one of the best health professionals I have had the pleasure of interacting with. His approach to injuries is different than most, as he looks at the body in its entirety to determine the root cause. This book provides a special opportunity for a glimpse into Mike's injury prevention and treatment methods. Any runner, from beginner to elite, should take advantage of the valuable information contained within!"

—Caleb Rhynard
3x NCAA Division 1 All-American Michigan State University
2x High School State Champion Track and Cross-Country
PRs: Mile 4:03, 5K 13:49, 10K 29:10

"Recurrent injury and setbacks riddled my high school career. When I started working with Mike, I was able to train pain-free, more consistently, and more efficiently. This also allowed me to compete at the NCAA DI level. My work with Mike not only helped my running, but also inspired me to become a physical therapist so I too could help runners reach their goals, and I still learn from him to this day."

—Adam Gilbert, DPT, CSCS, Jasper, IN

"Mike Swinger has been an invaluable resource for Shepherd Cross-Country and Track & Field Teams for several years. From treating athletes to designing drills and exercises, if we have a form or injury issue Mike is the first person we talk to. His knowledge of biomechanics, outside-the-box thinking and years of experience are a great combination in making runners healthier, more efficient, and faster."

—Carey Hammel, Shepherd Cross-Country and Track & Field
Girls Coach
MHSAA D3 Cross-Country State Champions - 2013
MHSAA D3 3200m Relay State Champions - 2014, 2015, 2017
MHSAA D3 800m Run State Champion - 2017
MITCA D3 Cross-Country Coach of the Year - 2013
MITCA D3 Cross-Country Coach of the Year Nominee - 2014,
2015, 2016
MITCA D3 Track & Field Coach of the Year Nominee - 2017
USATF Level 2 Certified Coach

"Mike Swinger has a gift of being able to quickly diagnose and treat runners of all abilities unlike that of anyone I have met. He talks often about the 'cranky muscle' and can quickly get to the source of a runner's problem, thereby helping them return to training and racing quickly. His book does a great job of helping one look beyond the point of pain and get to the cause of the problem. One of the hardest things about coaching is seeing an athlete not be able to do what they so greatly love. Mike's willingness to share and put into writing his knowledge on prevention and treatment make his book a must for all who wake up each day saying, 'It's a great day to run!'"

—**Laurens TenKate, Calvin Christian Cross-Country and Track Coach**
2011 National Coach of Year
2010 & 2011 Michigan Coach of Year
2011 Boys Spartan Elite Champions
2x Michigan Team Champions
2x Michigan State Team Runners-Up
Coached over 110 all-state cross-country and track athletes

"Mike Swinger's approach to physical therapy has changed the way my athletes view injuries. His preventative techniques and rehabilitation exercises reduce the amount of time lost due to injury and this book has helped us all to gain a better understanding of the biomechanics of running."

—**Kyle McKown, Clare Girls Cross-Country and Track & Field Coach**

"What makes six Harper family runners (including high school, collegiate, and marathon levels) travel thousands of miles over many years to visit physical therapist Mike Swinger? It's called top-notch injury prevention and rehabilitation. Mike is simply the best in our book."

—**Lisa Harper, Marathon Mission Founder, mother of three collegiate runners, 21-time marathon finisher**

"I began working with Mike Swinger about 10 years ago for a running-related injury that I could not find a solution to. Immediately I noticed that Mike had a different approach from anyone I had seen. Mike focuses on finding the root of the problem and fixing it instead of just treating the symptoms. Mike has helped me with my running form and has helped me become a better and healthier runner. As I continue to train and run competitively at age 41, I lean on Mike often for advice and help as issues pop up. As a cross-country and track coach, I have taken many runners with extensive issues to seek Mike's opinion. The number of athletes he has helped from our program is too numerous to count. As a program, we lean on Mike for individual help as well as countless activities in our daily routines to keep kids healthy and help them become better runners."

—Rick Cahoon, Shepherd Boys Cross-Country and Track & Field Coach, MHSAA Boys D3 Cross-Country State Champion, 2008

Runner's Fix

DIY Guide to Running Pain-Free

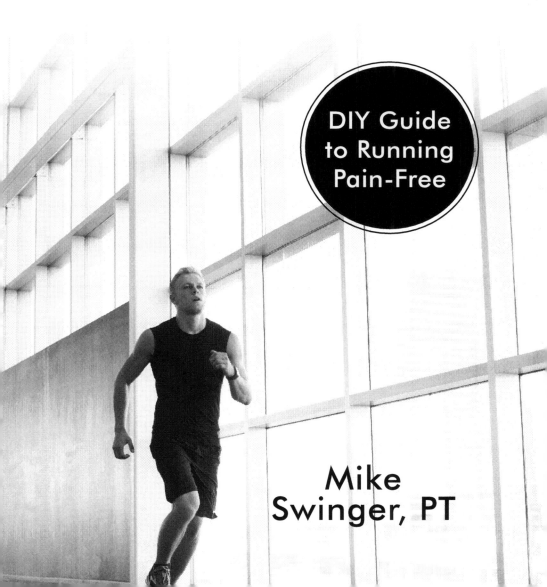

Mike
Swinger, PT

Runner's Fix
DIY Guide to Running Pain-Free
By Mike Swinger, PT © 2018

Print ISBN: 978-1-7327925-0-0
eBook ISBN: 978-1-7327925-1-7

Interior and Cover Design by: Fusion Creative Works, FusionCW.com
Photo Credits: Beautiful Life Photography
Photo Models: Cameron Versluis, Megan Yabani, Kate Wierenga

For more information, visit RunPhys.com

Published by Runphys, LLC

Printed in the United States of America

To any runner who sets a goal and strives for it,
may this book serve you well in your journey!

Contents

"Give me six hours
to chop down a tree and
I will spend the first four
sharpening the axe."

—Abraham Lincoln

Introduction

I wrote this book to help you become a better runner and avoid injuries. My hope is to give you the tools you need to manage many of the common issues runners deal with on a regular basis. In considering whether to put my thoughts and ideas in print, I was very reluctant for a time. My thought process was, why bother? So much information is out there already, I do not have much that is new or different to contribute.

Indeed, there is no shortage of information available today. Accessibility to that information is also unprecedented. The rise of availability and accessibility are good things, but the dark side is that accuracy and reliability are much more elusive. So, rather than rely on Dr. Google or Professor YouTube, this book is intended to be a reliable resource that has a helpful depth of information and is also easily accessible.

In today's online world, it takes very little to portray yourself as an "expert." While it would be great to say that every "expert" has attained their status organically, I cannot honestly believe that is the case anymore. As I launched my running blog in 2015, I could not help but compare it to other more popular websites and personalities. Unfortunately, the narrative for many of these "experts" goes something like this: "Look at me, I'm a superstar, these are the things I do to be successful so you should do these things too, so you can be a superstar like me." It is helpful to consider the examples of people who are successful, but it can also be dangerous to blindly follow every footstep. Also, the advice given is usually based on their own experiences and what has worked for them. We can learn from that, but their story is not likely to be your story.

My expertise in this area has little to do with my personal journey as a runner, but much more to do with the hundreds of runners I've had the privilege of working with in my career as a physical therapist thus far. Rather than write from the perspective of what has worked for me, this book is a distillation of what has worked for the many runners I have been able to help achieve their goals. This crowd ranges from first-time 5K runners to Ironman competitors and collegiate All-Americans.

This book is not intended to be a one-size-fits-all approach to fixing running issues. Rather, the information is designed to equip you to be proactive in taking care of your own body. To best use the tools listed in this book, start with the specific area where you seem to need the most work. For example, if shin splints are your concern, then start in the shin sections. If these do not seem to be effective, then start looking for clues in the muscles and joints above or below.

Perhaps an old ankle injury is an underlying cause. In this case, try the ankle exercises and see if that has an effect on your shins.

When it comes to the biomechanics of the body, the statement "Everything is connected" certainly holds true. Sorting out exactly how it is all connected can get very complicated. If you do not have a true biomechanics expert on speed-dial, then my recommendation is to start where you have the biggest issue, then gradually work your way up or down from there. If your knee tends to misbehave, start with exercises that address your knee. If those do not seem to get the job done, then assess how your hip and ankle are behaving according to the tests and exercises listed in this book. If you find an issue in your hip, then address that and see how it affects your knee. The understanding that the pain you are experiencing often has an underlying weakness or imbalance nearby is one of my most important messages.

Section One:

Laying the Foundations

Imagine a scenario where injuries didn't exist . . . pretty amazing, right? What could we accomplish if injuries were not a factor? The sky would be the limit. Sub-two-hour marathons, sub-three-minute miles, and other currently impossible feats would be normal if we could hammer workouts and train endlessly without risk of breaking down.

Unfortunately, our world doesn't work like that. We have certain laws of physics, nature, and human physiology that push back on our desires to push forward.

Now, imagine a scenario where each person is equipped to manage injuries that he or she sustains. This would be characterized by athletes that do NOT get shin splints two weeks into their cross-country season and marathon runners who do NOT break down as they are approaching peak mileage. What if you could detect the early signs that an injury may be around the corner, or better yet, proactively work to keep yourself in top form?

That is the purpose of this book. Most people see two paths for dealing with injuries. Either they rely on Dr. Google, which is cheap and accessible—but how reliable is it really?—or, they see their medical professional, which is usually not cheap and can often be inconvenient, especially if they have to wait weeks to get an appointment or the needed answers.

My hope is to provide another option. This book is intended to be a reliable source of information that is accessible and affordable. My hope is that at the first signs of your body misbehaving, you can be armed with the knowledge you need to get back on track quickly without it turning into a full-blown injury.

Disclaimer: If you have any suspicion that you need an appointment with your doctor, please pursue it. The exercises and suggestions included here are not intended to be a rehabilitation protocol and are not thorough enough nor individualized to function as a game plan for returning from injury.

Another side note: I certainly recommend using Google to look up anatomical terms that might not be immediately clear (italicized terms are defined in a glossary at the end of the book; others you may need to look up). It is safe to look up a picture of your "tibialis posterior" muscle to learn more about the location. But I discourage you from treating a Google search as the most authoritative source for diagnosing a potential injury.

With that being said, let us look at two hypothetical situations this book should be a resource for. Molly is a 16-year-old high school cross-country runner. She has been a runner for three years, though she dabbles in other sports and doesn't train year-round. Every fall, she begins experiencing medial (inside) shin pain about two to three weeks into her season. The pain isn't bad enough that she has to quit or go see her doctor. But it is bad enough that she can only do half the workouts, and often bikes instead of doing recovery and long runs. She is able to make it through the season but is often frustrated that she is hindered from improving on her personal record (PR).

Knowing her propensity for shin issues, if Molly committed to a few key exercises to work on at the beginning of summer, that would greatly increase her chances of staying strong all season and improving her PR.

Let us also consider Dave, who is a 45-year-old marathon runner. He has run two marathons in the past. Dave has faithfully followed a plan for building up mileage appropriately and always feels great for the first few months of training. However, hamstring and *glute* tightness always seems to rear its ugly head with about six weeks until race day. This causes him to cut his long runs short and dial back his midweek workouts, especially staying on flat surfaces. He is able to supplement swimming and elliptical workouts to keep cardio going but is frustrated by missing his runs when he had planned to be hitting peak mileage. He is able to complete his marathon, but often has to stop and stretch and again falls well short of qualifying for Boston.

Dave has done some cross-training and strength training in the off season but has not committed to a good stretching routine during the season. He would rather just lace up and go for a run. What if Dave had five minutes of targeted stretches in his daily routine that kept his muscles from getting cranky?

Both of our runners have searched YouTube and subscribed to a leading running magazine as sources of information. But neither of them felt the need to see their doctor, as their issues resolve when they stop running.

Again, the goal of this book is to fill in the gap that is left between their online searches and seeking direct medical advice. This is intended to be a reliable resource to prevent issues from arising or get you back on track when issues first start to surface.

The majority of the book is divided into chapters based on the different body parts and common issues that arise. Please appreciate that the suggestions for exercises and assessments are attempts to paint with a broad stroke. Your situation may not nicely fall into one of the categories discussed! I recommend that you consider the nearby body parts as well. For instance, if you have struggled with medial shin splints, then also consider the factors that affect your calves, feet, and ankles, as your situation may be more broadly based. Or if your hips have been problematic, also consider your low back, quads, and hamstrings as potential contributors.

By considering more factors and experimenting with these suggestions, you can design your own routine to best meet your needs. A runner armed with better knowledge of her own body is a very confident runner indeed. A runner who knows his body well can also understand better how to correct other issues that arise along the way. A runner who knows her body well can also tell when she needs to seek medical advice because attempts to course-correct have not worked, and she is confident that she has truly tried everything first!

Types of Injuries

For the sake of our discussion, my approach is that there are two basic kinds of injuries: mechanical and progressive. Mechanical injuries have an obvious one-time cause. A sprained ankle is an example of a mechanical injury. In the medical world we use the phrase MOI (mechanism of injury). Typically with running, mechanical injuries are the minority, though we do see sprained ankles, foot fractures after a misstep, and injuries from falling. With mechanical injuries, it's best to seek medical advice to determine the extent of injury. The content of this book is not geared toward dealing with these types of acute injuries as there is typically tissue damage that needs further care.

However, underlying imbalances can often make you susceptible to mechanical injuries. Chronic ankle rolls and recurring hamstring pulls fall into this category. If you have sustained a mechanical injury, it is worthwhile to sort out any factors that got you there once the acute injury is past. For example, if you have pulled your hamstring, usually some sort of hip *muscle imbalance* contributed to that injury. If you suspect your mechanical injury may have underlying factors, then this book is for you.

Progressive issues are what most runners deal with. Many runners do not even like to consider themselves "injured" if they are unable to run as they want to. Rather than argue about semantics, we will use the phrases injury and injured as the extreme ends of a spectrum. So one end of the spectrum is characterized by all parts feeling perfectly healthy. The other end is a full-blown injury (think stress fracture or debilitating pain with walking). Let us consider that the vast middle section of this spectrum is characterized by various levels of crankiness in your muscles and joints. If you are not sure where you actually fall on this spectrum then please get some advice from a trusted medical professional. Better safe than sorry!

Progressive issues occur due to accumulated stress in any given area. Consider that pain is your body's attempt to get your attention. Quite often, the area of pain is overstressed due to the misbehaving of other body parts. We will get into the common compensation patterns for each area later. Our bodies are designed to withstand a certain amount of stress, but too much can cause inflammation and/or physiological breakdown of muscles, tendons, *fascia,* bones, ligaments, etc. Usually by the time we realize a muscle is cranky, this process is well underway.

Ten-Percent Rule and Physiological Adaptation

You've likely heard of the "10-percent rule" for building up mileage. This is a good guideline to follow anytime you plan to make significant changes to the miles you plan to run. In addition to compensation patterns being a risk factor for injury, attempting to build up your mileage or intensity too quickly runs the same risks.

Your body is designed to adapt on multiple levels. On a physiological level, your bones are constantly being broken down and rebuilt according to the stresses placed on them. Bones are not solid and consistent throughout. Rather, they have developed to be strong for the unique needs of each body part. (Look up the phrase "bone trabeculae" sometime to get a more in-depth look at this concept.) The important thing to remember is that bones are living and changing tissues. When you stress them, they adapt to that stress. When you stress them too much or too quickly in a new way, the rebuilding process cannot keep up. Follow that pattern for a few weeks and you are risking a stress fracture.

When it comes to soft tissues (any body part that is not bone), you still need to be aware of building up in the proper amounts. Your ligaments, tendons, fascia, and *joint capsules* are designed to stretch and bounce back (think strong rubber bands). These structures are passive, in that they cannot contract or act according to their own volition. Rather, these structures have elastic properties that depend on outside forces. Still, these structures can adapt over time the way bones do. It is important to place just enough stress on them to get adaptation, but not too much too quickly so that they get cranky. Crankiness in these tissues is essentially where we get a lot of the "itises" from (tendinitis, bursitis, etc.). Your body's response to increased stress in these areas is inflammation. A little inflammation that is gracefully cleared out is a normal part of the stress/response process. When inflammation accumulates in an area, then it can really mess with the healthy function of the tissues. An example of this is an inflamed patellar tendon insertion that is inhibiting proper activation of the quadriceps.

Your passive soft tissues also need time to adapt. The adaptation is simply the tissues (ligaments, tendons, fascia, joint capsules) getting used to the number of times your foot hits the ground. The greatest shock they withstand is the force of the ground pushing up into your body. If you plan to strike the ground 90 times per minute for 60 minutes (5,400 times!), then you better progressively build up so your body can absorb that many impacts without all those tight rubber bands breaking down.

The 10-percent rule is important for muscles also. In order for your muscles to be happy, you need the fibers to be strong enough and accustomed to the number of contractions needed to run (1,300-2,700 steps for a 5K, upwards of 20,000 for a marathon!). In the same way as your other parts, the muscle fibers need time to adapt to the impact. This impact "loads" the muscles, which initiates a contraction. The ability to load and respond is a movement skill that your muscles need to practice many times over to become efficient. Also, your muscles require a lot of oxygen and nutrition to work. How efficiently your muscles are able to use their resources will improve progressively as they gain fitness.

It is easy to ignore the role of nerve health as you aspire to build up mileage, but you need to understand how fatigue affects your nerves. Your muscles do not fire unless the nerves are telling them to. The process of nerve-muscle stimulation is one that also will acclimate to stresses placed on it. Consider it this way: the nerve stimulates the muscles by spitting out little neurotransmitters (NTs), then sucking them back up and spitting them out again. At some point, that process will "fatigue," causing the muscle to not re-ceive the localized stimulation it needs to keep firing. When this happens, your brain will pick up on that and try to get more muscle recruitment somewhere else. If this keeps happening, then you have the beginnings of a compensation pattern, or a muscle imbalance. Essentially, a compensation pattern is your *neuromuscular* system figuring out another way to get the job done. Over time, this will cause stress to accumulate more quickly in the areas that are overworking.

Importance of Proper Form

Understanding what proper form is can be somewhat elusive, with various "experts" giving advice on how to run properly. Quite often, ideal form is talked about with rather dogmatic terms and techniques that have a compelling narrative and make sense on the surface, but unfortunately fail to consider the deeper physiology of your body, as well as your individuality. While it is important to understand the underlying principles at work, spend five minutes watching the elites on TV and you will see variations in how they run.

So rather than get too intense about the nuts and bolts of proper running form, our discussion will best be kept at a more philosophical level. Essentially, running with proper form amounts to moving from point A to B in the most efficient manner. How that is accomplished is quite complicated on a biomechanical/subconscious level.

Think about proper form as your joints being in their ideal place at any given moment, to minimize stress on the soft tissues and position your muscles to be able to fire effectively and without inhibition. Again, that is still rather abstract, but if we start there, then it helps frame any conversations we have about how your feet should strike the ground, or ideal cadence, or barefoot running, or should you tilt your pelvis or suck in your belly button or squeeze your glutes, or what should your arms be doing, etc.

Rather than give a full dissertation about running form, (which could easily be a book of its own!) I think it is more helpful to understand that your form is your body expressing itself through running. Each person has his or her own unique body which is going to behave differently when in motion. If you have tight *hip flexors*, that is going to show up somehow. If you have weakness in your forefoot, that is going to show up also. If you have glute and core weakness, you better believe that will show up somehow!

All too often, attempts to "fix" your running form focus on the expression, rather than the underlying factor. I believe that if there is something about your form that needs improving, the best place to start is with addressing the flexibility and strength of the key areas. Once these are improving, then form drills are helpful and necessary to retrain the total body neuromuscular patterns.

Let us touch on a few key principles for running with good form. First, minimize over-striding. You may or may not be familiar with that term. Essentially, it refers to where your foot lands relative to the rest of your body. If your foot lands way out in front, that creates significant inefficiency in your form. It is the same as hitting the brakes every time you run!

Second, eliminate extraneous movements in your knees, hips, core, and upper body. This can look like excessive knee wobble, or hip drop, or hips swinging out, or forward trunk lean, or arms rotating too heavily. There are other possibilities, but these all indicate weakness or tightness that is causing your body to load and respond inefficiently.

Third, find your ideal cadence. There are schools of thought that are touting 90 steps/min as the absolute best for everyone. I disagree with this as an absolute. It is best to be in the neighborhood (80-100), but there is too much variability in runners' bodies to be able to put a firm number on it. Rather, each person needs to consider his or her own body and experience to figure this out. A six-foot-five-inch male with a 36-inch inseam is not going to run with the same cadence as a five-foot-one-inch female. It is foolish to lump them in the same box.

Consider two children swinging on two different length swings. The child on the longer swing will not be able to complete as many back and forths in the same amount of time as the child on the shorter swing. There is a natural rhythm that comes with the length. If the child on the longer swing attempts to kick and pump his legs as quickly as the other child, he will end up falling on his face. In the same way, the length and skill of our bodies creates a natural cadence rhythm. It can certainly adapt with practice, but will never be the same as someone who is built differently and has a different physiology.

Another way to look at cadence is to think about how much time your foot spends on the ground with each step. Typically, the less time you can spend on the ground with each step will result in less susceptibility to injury. But this also has diminishing returns. A typical distance runner spends between 0.2-0.3 seconds on the ground with each step. It may be beneficial to try shaving off a couple hundredths of a second but try to go too low, and you will sacrifice your efficiency somewhere.

Last, your foot should strike the ground in a way that allows your entire body to load and respond efficiently. For some people, this may be a forefoot strike. For others, a slight heel strike is the best way to go. Still others operate best with a midfoot landing. There are pros and cons to each type. Please do not assume that what works best for one person will work best for you. Rather, if you focus on avoiding over-striding and running in a way that is most efficient for the rest of your body, your foot strike will find its own happy place. To arbitrarily decide to adopt a certain type of striking pattern has the potential to hijack the load-response pattern in the rest of your body.

Importance of
Proper Flexibility

Flexibility certainly gets plenty of press, but how many of us truly pursue it intently? I certainly didn't for many years and suspect that the majority of us are guilty as well. If we understand what flexibility is and why it is important, then we have potential to change our ways.

Essentially, flexibility is the ability to lengthen your muscles under load and return to normal length. Your muscles will lack flexibility when you don't use them through their length, or when your muscles are lacking the confidence to be stable into their further lengths.

All muscle tightness is not created equal. Often, your muscles are structurally tight, lacking the length they need to allow for movement. Tight hamstrings affecting your ability to touch your toes is the classic example. In these situations, aggressive sustained stretching is often very beneficial to gain length, though it is a long hard road that most people are not willing to put the work in.

Quite often, where flexibility breaks down stems from a muscle's own sense of self-preservation rather than passive tightness. As a muscle lengthens toward the end range, its strength capacity declines and quality of movement is compromised. If a muscle does not have enough strength to pull itself out of a deep stretch, the muscle will be reluctant to allow itself to be lengthened that far. You are then left with a muscle that has the length, but feels the need to protect itself. This muscle is going to behave as if it is lacking flexibility. With muscles that are behaving this way, it is necessary to stretch, but *dynamic stretching* is more effective and needs to be complemented by strength and stability work in the lengthened ranges.

One benefit of proper flexibility is that your muscles work more efficiently. As you run, your muscles lengthen and shorten. Your body weight must still be supported as muscles lengthen when your foot strikes the ground. This is the concept of "lengthen under load." Your muscles have passive elastic properties to them, as well as active contractile fibers. Essentially, if you can properly lengthen a muscle under load, then the muscle is able to take advantage of the free potential energy the elastic fibers provide. Your muscles work much more efficiently when they are taking advantage of this free potential energy. Picture someone jumping as high as he can. Which scenario can he jump higher from: standing straight up or quick squat first? Obviously, a quick squat first to load the muscles. In the same way, your muscles are much happier to work when you load them before asking them to return the favor.

Another benefit of proper flexibility is for body awareness, aka *proprioception*. Distance runners are notorious for being deficient in this area. Your muscles have individual, subconscious awareness that gives feedback to your entire neuromuscular system. Your conscious brain says "run!" and then your body takes over. When muscles are happy and healthy, the feedback is clear and precise. When your muscles detect something is wrong, a monkey wrench is thrown into the whole system. A tight muscle can cause surrounding muscles to be affected because of the dysfunctional signals it is sending to your brain. Your brain then interprets these signals and has to make decisions on how to overcome a tight muscle. You better believe this affects how you run and how happily the rest of your body works.

Importance of Proper Strength

Runners do not need to be bodybuilders, but they do need enough strength to function properly. So what does that look like? Think 2-3 times your body weight for a split second on each foot. Every time your foot hits the ground, you need enough strength to efficiently manage your own body weight, plus the effects of momentum and gravity. Physics 101 says that F=MA, or force equals mass times acceleration. Physics 102 says that for every force there's an equal and opposite force. With every stride that you take, there is a collision of forces between the ground and your body. The ground is going to be fine. It is not going anywhere. Your body, however, needs enough strength to manage the incoming load (the ground pushing back up on you) without compromising alignment.

If your strength is not able to be wielded quickly and properly when you land, that will show up in some way. One common way is increased ground contact time. The typical distance runner spends between 0.2-0.3 seconds with her foot on the ground each stride. During that time, the shock of the ground needs to be fully absorbed and pushed back off again. If her strength is sufficient, then the proper muscles absorb that force in the proper way and turn that input force into an output force in order to push her body off for the next step. Then the cycle repeats itself a few thousand more times!

There are several predictable patterns of weakness which we will get into as we address common injuries in the next section. Simply put, a weak muscle will not properly absorb the incoming force with each stride. The result is more stress on the neighboring muscles to pick up the slack from the offending muscle. In order to recruit other muscles, your body will have to compromise form and alignment to accomplish this.

With every step you take, your body and brain are trying to figure out how to move forward as happily as possible. If every muscle is contributing as it should, everyone is happy. If a muscle is slacking, then your body has to figure out how to make up for that. This compensation will cause another muscle to overwork. Your body is pretty intent on keeping your face from hitting the floor, so your subconscious will readily find another muscle to pick up the slack. In this scenario, you have the beginnings of a muscle imbalance, which will likely lead to an overuse injury at some point.

Again, with every stride you take, your form is an expression of your body's habits. If you have a habit of using your muscles properly, your form will look and feel good. If you have weakness somewhere, that will show up in your form. Picture the ground reaction force as it travels through your foot and calf, up through your quads and hamstrings, and into your hip. Right around your hip and lower core (think below your belly button), that force should be mostly absorbed. When that's the case, your upper body is able to stay relaxed and quietly helps to leverage your hips along. If the hips and lower core are not strong enough, the ground reaction force continues to travel upward until your body can recruit enough other muscles to stop that rampant force from traveling further. In order to do this, your upper body will have to move differently to recruit these extra muscles. This is one example of how weakness affects your form and efficiency!

There are many other ways that weakness plagues runners that we will get into in the next section. Glute and core weakness are common areas of weakness. Planks and lunges are often a great way to start but are seldom sufficient to truly build proper core strength. Many times, subtle patterns of weakness are present in your feet, lower legs, quads, and hamstrings. When these are present, it will cause misalignment from the ground up. In these scenarios, your hips and core don't stand a chance to fire properly since they are trying to work from an unstable platform.

Strengthening is very important for all your muscles but is not as simple as doing isolated bulking up of each muscle. It is more important that each muscle can quickly respond appropriately to each force input, as well as turn it around quickly into a force output. It doesn't take a bulky muscle to do this! If you can squat five hundred pounds, but it takes you two full seconds to go up and down, this will not help your running strength very much. You would be better off to do a few squats at a lighter weight to develop form, but then progress into single-leg exercises and do them quickly (think single-leg step-ups and plyometrics). If you have to choose, pick a quick and efficient muscle over a bulky muscle every time.

So, how much strength do you need to be a good runner? Enough to manage your body weight and ground reaction forces efficiently, to avoid compensation. The trick then becomes how to develop that type of strength and make it last over the course of your event. If your muscle is strong for the first five minutes and then fatigues, it will cause imbalances and overuse elsewhere.

Section Two:

Common Runner Injuries

This section is dedicated to the injuries and cranky spots that occur commonly with runners. If you suspect that you have an injury of any severity, please get it checked out by your trusted medical provider. This book is not intended to replace direct medical care. Rather, the information in this section is helpful for keeping you tuned up so injuries do not occur.

When is the best time to use these exercises? Every day! The exercises listed in the following sections are designed to keep your body "tuned up." So often, overuse injuries occur because muscles fatigue and fall into imbalanced compensated patterns. Without being proactive, your body will more quickly fall into these imbalanced patterns every time you push your body. This can lead to imbalance being the default pattern your muscles work under. Not good!

So rather than drift down that path, it is best to perform your key exercises every day before you run in order to keep your muscles properly tuned up and balanced.

Which exercises are the key ones for you? That's what the rest of this book is dedicated to. As you read each section, reflect on your own story and see which part or parts resonate with you. This will help you determine what exercises will best address your unique needs. Also, do not be surprised if your top exercises change over time.

How do you perform each exercise? As you prepare for each run, dynamic stretches are typically the best way to work on flexibility. Dynamic (moving) stretches wake up the neuromuscular system and get blood flowing. Typically 30-60 seconds is sufficient for dynamic stretches. Static (holding a lengthened position) stretches inhibit the neuromuscular connections and can compromise proprioception, so they are usually not recommended prior to running. After running, static stretches can be a crucial part of your recovery routine. Often static stretches require 3-5 minutes of sustained hold to create an effect. The stretches in this book are described from a dynamic stretching standpoint. The same positions will be effective for *static stretching*, but simply held in the deepest position demonstrated.

The strengthening exercises are best performed for 15-30 reps prior to running. The goal of these exercises is to awaken and stimulate the muscles that tend to get lazy. The goal of these exercises is NOT to reach a fatigue or failure point, so please use your judgement with how many repetitions you perform. A simple exercise like back rocking can take 30-50 reps at times, but a more challenging exercise such as the "twisty supermans" may get the job done in 10 reps. The important thing with these exercises is that the targeted area is more awake and alert after you are done.

With all that being said, let us dive into each area of the body where runners tend to hurt. Short videos of each exercise are available at RunPhys.com/injuryprevention.

Low Back: The Crossroads of Forces Between Upper and Lower Body

Let us start with the most complicated area. The low back is a crossroads for the entire body. Because of this, a lot of stress travels through this area. In the low back and lower core, the forces and movements pivot and transfer between upper and lower body. This is one of the reasons that core strength is such an important topic.

There are several reasons that runners develop low back pain. Simply put, core weakness and imbalance between the hip muscles is a big underlying factor. Quite often, tightness in the psoas muscle is present, along with weakness of the lower abdominals. The psoas muscles originate along either side of your low back, extending from your upper lumbar spine, running through the back of your abdominal cavity, down to the groin. Your psoas also has small attachments onto your diaphragm. Your psoas muscles will tend to overwork when the abdominals are not holding their proper position. It's also very easy to overuse your psoas and underutilize your abdominals when performing many core exercises (crunches, planks, bicycles, flutter kicks, etc.).

Quick anatomy lesson: The psoas muscles are part of the hip flexor muscle group and are usually the strongest of the group. Hip flexion is a sagittal plane motion (forward/backward), but the psoas muscles also have a very strong transverse plane (rotation) contribution. The joints of your low back are not designed to rotate very well. In fact, the joints and discs of your low back get cranky very quickly if the muscles are not keeping them stable. If there is imbalance between any of the muscles in your core, excessive motion in your low back is often the result. Over time this can cause weakness in the supporting ligaments of your low back, pelvis, and sacrum.

Another key muscle is the iliacus, which is the partner in crime of the psoas (together they often are referred to as the iliopsoas). The iliacus muscle originates on the inside of your pelvis, then follows the psoas down into the groin. Because of its location, it has a significant role in stabilizing your *sacroiliac joint.*

One of the hallmark signs of low back issues due to hip flexor tightness is discomfort with bending backward. One of the simplest things you can do to address these low back issues is to stretch your hip flexors. The picture demonstrates the position to generally stretch your hip flexors. Once your hip flexors are loosened up, it is helpful to fire up your abdominals using back rocking.

Back-bending self-test: If bending backward is painful or stiff, hip flexor tightness is likely a contributor.

Kneeling hip flexor stretch: Start in a kneeling position, then drive forward with your hips until a stretch is felt in the front of the thigh of the kneeling leg. Gently pulse forward and backward 20-30x, being careful not to arch your back.

Back rocking: Lay on your back and grasp both knees. Rock forward and backward, attempting to get your hips off the floor and driving your knees upward at least 20-30x.

Hamstring tightness and/or weakness can also be a contributor to low back issues. Your hamstrings are a group of three muscles that originate off your sit bone (ischial tuberosity) and extend to just below your knee. The hamstrings should work in harmony with your other hip and core muscles to keep your pelvis in proper alignment. When the hamstrings misbehave, it causes your hips to move incorrectly every time your foot hits the ground. This will create motion in your low back that is extraneous and inefficient (picture your friend who runs with an upper body swagger—not you, of course!).

If you have discomfort or tightness with touching your toes, chances are good that hamstring tightness is a contributor for you. Stretching your hamstrings is best done with a slight bend in your knee and paying careful attention to keeping your low back rigid. Ensure that the movement comes from your hips, not your low back. More often than not, when attempting hamstring stretches, we tend to flex and move more from our low back rather than our hips. Most common hamstring stretches are done incorrectly, which can propagate a dysfunctional pattern. Once you've loosened up the hamstrings, single-leg deadlifts are a good way to develop proper strength with this pattern.

Hamstring stretch: Prop one foot on a chair with knee slightly bent. Arch your low back, then gently pivot forward at your hips until a stretch is felt in the back of the thigh. Gently pulse hips forward and backward 20-30x.

Single-leg deadlifts: Balance on one leg, then lean forward with your upper body reaching straight forward. At the same time, raise the rear leg up, attempting to get parallel to the ground, 10-15x on each leg.

Another common cause of low back issues is the joints of your sacrum (tailbone) and pelvis falling out of alignment. While running, your sacrum is designed to rotate a little between the right and left sides of your pelvic bones. This is normal and healthy to have subtle movements taking place in these bones with every step you take. What can often happen is that the sacrum will get stuck rotated to the right or left. Also, one side of the pelvis can get stuck rotated forward, backward, or other directions. When your joints are out of alignment at rest, pain often results due to the attaching ligaments being stressed or the joint surfaces themselves having too much friction. Pain with rotation can be an indicator for joints being out of alignment.

*Standing rotation self-test: Rotate your upper body
side to side. If either direction elicits pain,
joint misalignment is likely a factor.*

Misalignments like these happen regularly and are usually the result of imbalance somewhere in the hips. Many
times, the joints are locked up enough that you need to
consult your medical provider, who can perform hands-on
treatments to realign. Sometimes you can take care of it
yourself. Along with stretching your hip flexors as shown
previously, the pigeon pose stretch is the first one to try.
Usually you'll find that one hip is tighter than the other with
this stretch. If that is the case, there is a good chance that
your hips have been moving asymmetrically, which is probably the cause for joints going out of alignment. Once you
have improved your flexibility, it is important to build up
strength throughout the needed ranges. Quite often, exercises such as clamshells and single-leg bridges will be
recommended for strengthening hips. These are a good
start, but ultimately your muscles need to be lengthened

under load before returning to neutral. Twisty supermans are an excellent way to strengthen your hips throughout the entire range.

Twisty supermans: Start in single-leg deadlift position, then pivot at your hips to rotate your entire upper body and raised leg up and down, 10-15x. It is okay to hold on with one hand if you have trouble balancing.

*Pigeon pose stretch: Start in hands-and-knees position,
then place one leg behind the other and rotate front leg
90 degrees. Lean your weight onto the front leg
and gently rotate your hips 20-30x.*

Again, the low back usually misbehaves because of imbalances between the hips and core muscles. The pain that you feel can come either from overworked muscles, which will likely feel tight and achy in nature, or from joints and ligaments under stress. This will likely feel more localized and sharp. There are many different patterns of imbalance that can cause low back issues. Some are more rare and complicated, in which case you will likely need to see your medical professional. But the majority of imbalances fall into the patterns mentioned in this chapter.

Upper Back: Do Not Let This Area Restrict Your Stride

Upper back issues are often due to flexibility deficits in the postural muscles, and restricted motion of the spine and ribcage. With running, there is frequently weakness in lower parts of the core, which causes overuse of the upper core muscles (think diaphragm and the muscles that stabilize your ribcage).

Spending two to three minutes of quality time with a foam roller is one of the best ways to address tightness in your upper back. Stretches for your upper body are also very helpful.

Thoracic foam roller: Start with knees bent and foam roller placed across the middle of your back. Gently roll up and down, allowing your spine and ribcage to relax over top the foam roller. Move slowly, 20-30x.

Prayer stretch: From hands-and-knees position, sit backward toward your heels, and drive your head down toward the ground. Hold this position for at least 30 seconds, then slide one hand underneath the other and back, 20-30x. Repeat with the other hand.

Wall thoracic stretch: Standing next to a wall, hold onto the wall by reaching overhead with hand furthest away from the wall. Then take the free hand and reach as far forward and backward as possible, 20-30x. Repeat with the other hand.

Along with these stretches, it is also critical to address any core or hip imbalances you have. Since running is primarily a lower body activity, most issues with your upper body are a direct result of imbalance in your lower half. Think about what your arms and shoulders do while running. Essentially, you move your arms to counterbalance your legs. Have you ever tried running with your right arm and right leg advancing at the same time? That would be pretty awkward and inefficient. So, if your upper body is not happy, make sure to address hip and core issues along with any stretches or foam rolling that you do.

Side note: If you are not sure where to start, your arms will often be a tattle tale for the lower body. For instance, if your arms tend to ride high, chances are you do not have proper strength and flexibility of your lateral hips. Get your hips behaving and see if it is easier to keep your arms more relaxed. If your arms rotate a lot, causing your hands to cross the midline of your body, chances are that your hips and core are not strong enough with rotational movements. Address those and see if that cleans up your arm movements and makes life happier for your upper body.

Posterior Hip: Sacroiliac, Piriformis, and Glutes, Oh My!

Pain in the posterior hip is usually caused by tightness in the glute med or piriformis. Less frequently, the pain can come from the hip capsule itself (the ligaments that hold the ball in the socket), other deep small muscles, or the SI (sacroiliac) joint. It is very common for weakness to be present in the glute max and parts of the glute med and min. What often happens is that the glutes become weak in certain directions, causing the muscles to tighten up in other directions.

In order to address glute tightness, try the pigeon pose stretch along with a foam roller or tennis ball directly to the tight area for 2-3 minutes. Follow this up with strengthening your hips using curtsy lunges.

Pigeon pose stretch: Start in hands-and-knees position, then place one leg behind the other and rotate front leg 90 degrees. Lean your weight onto the front leg and gently rotate your hips, 20-30x.

Curtsy lunges: From standing position, step backward and across before lunging downward, 10-15x.

Less frequently, the SI joint can be a source of posterior hip pain. If you suspect this may be the case, check the flexibility of your hips using the *FABER test.*

FABER test: Lie on your back with one knee bent upward. Let your knee fall out to the side. If one side is tighter than the other or painful, it is a sign of restriction in your hip or SI joint.

If one hip is tighter than the other, that can be a sign that your SI joint is not moving properly. Do not be surprised if the side that is not hurting is the tighter side! Often one side of the SI will become restricted, causing the other side to become hypermobile. This will cause aggravation of the SI ligaments and piriformis muscle. In order to address SI restriction, perform the kneeling adductor stretch and kneeling iliacus stretch. Twisty superman squats are a great way to work on balance and stability of your SI joints.

Kneeling adductor stretch: Kneeling on one leg, rotate the upper leg 90 degrees until it is perpendicular to the kneeling leg. Keep your hips in line with the upper leg and gently drive your hips toward the upper foot to stretch the inner thigh, 20-30x.

Kneeling iliacus stretch: In kneeling position, gently slide your front leg out to the side 6-12 inches. Next, rotate your rear leg outward as far as you can. Gently drive your hips straight forward, 20-30x.

Twisty superman squats: Balance on one leg and reach forward with hands and upper body. Next rotate your hips and upper body upward, allow rear leg to counterbalance your upper body. In this position, perform single-leg squat 10-15x, paying careful attention to keeping hips rotated upward and not allowing your knee to dip inward.

Anterior-Medial Hip: Simple Groin Strain or Worse?

Pain in the anterior-medial hip or groin area is usually caused by tightness or strain of one of the muscles. Oftentimes there is a sharp or pinching feeling in the front of the hip. The muscles in this area that are most involved are the iliopsoas, pectineus (groin muscle), rectus femoris (central quad), or the adductors (inner thigh). Usually there is an underlying imbalance that causes one of these muscles to become cranky. The imbalance can be as simple as weak lower abs with tight and overworked hip flexors. But it can also be more complicated as well, including the hip flexors fighting over who gets to do what.

Over time this can turn into inflammation of the muscles, bursitis, or inflammation of the front of the hip capsule (the ligaments that hold the ball in the socket). Pain in this area is best addressed with gentle stretching to the hip flexors and adductors followed by hip scoops. As with any other issue, core/hip imbalances can be a big factor, so do not neglect doing your work there as well.

Kneeling hip flexor stretch: Start in a kneeling position, then drive forward with your hips until a stretch is felt in the front of the thigh of the kneeling leg. Gently pulse forward and backward 20-30x, being careful not to arch your back.

Hip scoops: Start in kneeling position, then raise up into tall kneeling position by leading with your hips and keeping spine in neutral, 10-20x.

Kneeling adductor stretch: Kneeling on one leg, rotate the upper leg 90 degrees until it is perpendicular to the kneeling leg. Keep your hips in line with the upper leg and gently drive your hips toward the upper foot to stretch the inner thigh, 20-30x.

Anterior-Lateral Hip: Is That Muscle Named After a Coffee Drink?

Pain in the anterior-lateral hip is usually strain or tightness in the tensor fascia latae (TFL) muscle. No, that is not a coffee drink—it is the real name of a real muscle! This muscle is often problematic when it misbehaves, for several reasons. First, it attaches directly onto your iliotibial (IT) band and is the biggest influencer of your IT band. Any tightness or weakness in the TFL is going to put the IT band in an awkward position.

Second, the TFL is a hip flexor, which means that it should nicely blend in with the other hip flexors to swing your leg forward. Tightness in the TFL will cause you to change the way your hip swings forward, which makes life more difficult for your other hip and core muscles and can also change the position of your foot and knee at the moment of impact.

Lastly, tightness or overuse of the TFL will inhibit the glutes. The TFL along with your glute min and med work to stabilize your hip when it is planted on the ground (collectively they are referred to as the abductors). The three *hip abductors* work together in the frontal plane of motion (side-to-side), so they should always get along, right? In the other planes of motion however, they are antagonists. The TFL wants to internally rotate the hip, the glutes want to externally rotate. The TFL is a hip flexor; the glutes are hip extensors.

With hip and knee issues, many will say to "strengthen the glutes!" And this is generally sound advice. What you need to consider, however, is that if there is already an imbalanced relationship in this area, then it is very easy to compensate and continue overusing your TFL. Try this simple self-test: lie on your side with your legs straight and raise your top leg up into the air. Does it drift forward into hip flexion? Chances are that your TFL is doing more of the work then it is supposed to and bullying your glutes in this direction. Still lying on your side, if your hip did indeed flex a little, see if you can keep your leg up, but bring it back into extension, without your hips rolling backward. Pretty challenging, right? Left to themselves, your muscles will continue imbalanced unless you are proactive in making them play nice together.

Side-lying hip abduction test: Lying on your side, raise your top leg straight up. If your leg drifts forward (left) or your hips roll backward, these are indicators of imbalance between glutes and TFL.

So the challenge really becomes how to get them to play nice together. The first step is to stretch the TFL followed by properly performed glute exercises. Simple side planks and side bridges are a great place to start. Pay close attention to your hips to ensure they stay neutral, not letting them drift backward or rotate. Strengthening your *hip external rotators* will also help restore balance. Once you are comfortable holding a side plank, kick the upper leg high into the air and do 20 backward circles.

Kneeling TFL stretch: Start in kneeling position, then slide front foot across your body 6-12 inches. Raise the same arm of the kneeling leg, then gently drive forward with your hips, 20-30x.

Side plank: Lay on your side propped on your elbow. Bridge upward with your hips, keeping your hips and spine in a straight line. Bridge up and down, 15x. Or, simply hold the side plank position for 30-60 seconds while kicking your upper leg up and down, forward and backward, and rotations.

The TFL often responds well to direct deep massage work using a tennis ball, foam roller, or the touch of a trusted practitioner. Also, do not hesitate to add in the suggested exercises for the posterior hip as these issues often overlap.

Lateral Knee and IT Band: Is Rolling the Only Option?

Before blaming any lateral knee issues on the knee itself, make sure you point some fingers at the hip. Quite often the knee takes the brunt of a misbehaving hip. Once you have addressed any hip issues, then you can turn your attention to the knee itself.

Usually pain in the lateral knee comes from the area where the IT band inserts onto the knee. You may have heard the term "IT band friction syndrome" referring to this type of pain. This area has been up for debate recently regarding where the pain is coming from and how best to address it. Some say not to foam roll because the IT band does not have the capacity to lengthen. Indeed, the IT band is not able to lengthen, but we can accomplish other things by using the foam roller. Directly underneath most of the IT band is a large muscle called the vastus lateralis (VL), or the lateral quad. During normal movements, there should be gliding of the IT band over the top of the VL, but oftentimes the fascia between the two becomes gnarled up. This is when things get cranky. Any tightness in the TFL (see previous section) or the VL can contribute to lateral knee issues.

Along with pain coming from the VL/IT band interface, it can also come from a little bony prominence on the outside of the knee. When your knee bends and straightens past 30 degrees, there is potential for a rubbing or plucking to occur. Regardless of the exact structure where the pain is coming from, the approach doesn't change much. Stretches for your lateral hip are the places to start. From there, get comfortable going slowly on your foam roller for two to three minutes.

ITB foam roller: Prop yourself on one elbow, with hips off the ground and roller in the middle of your lateral thigh. Using your upper leg to stabilize and moderate amount of body weight, place your foot on the ground in front. Slowly roll up and down, being careful to avoid the bony part of the outside of your hip and knee, 2-3 minutes.

Pigeon pose stretch: Start in hands-and-knees position, then place one leg behind the other and rotate front leg 90 degrees. Lean your weight onto the front leg and gently rotate your hips, 20-30x.

Kneeling TFL stretch: Start in kneeling position, then slide front foot across your body 6-12 inches. Raise the same arm of the kneeling leg, then gently drive forward with your hips, 20-30x.

Many times, there is associated weakness in the medial quad, aka vastus medialis oblique (VMO). In order to help balance out the medial and lateral quads, perform wide split squats.

Wide split squats: In lunge position, widen your feet approximately shoulder width. Squat straight down and up 15x, being careful to keep hips facing forward and not allowing knees to dip inward.

There are other causes of lateral knee pain that are somewhat rare in runners. One cause is injury or inflammation in the lateral collateral ligament (LCL). This is often caused by direct impact or twisting trauma to the ankle or knee. At times, the fibula bone (outside of lower leg) can be moving improperly. This can cause the LCL, IT band, or lateral hamstring insertion to be inflamed. If these descriptions of more rare situations seem to resonate with you, then try addressing it via the suggestions for calf and ankle issues in the coming sections. But these situations also may require a little rest and a call to your friendly neighborhood physical therapist.

Anterior Knee and Patellofemoral: Keep the Kneecap Tracking Properly

The anterior knee often becomes cranky due to tightness in the quads, specifically the rectus femoris (RF) and vastus intermedius (VI), also known as the central quads. The anterior knee can also become painful when the patella is not tracking properly within the groove. Every time you bend and extend your knee, your patella will glide up and down over top of the femur. The motion is not perfectly straight, but rather slightly C-shaped. The usual dysfunctions in this area involve tightness of the central quads and weakness of the VMO. The VMO attaches more directly onto the patella and thus has more influence on the tracking of the patella then the other three quads. Also, the angle at which the muscle fibers are oriented is significantly different than the other three.

Unfortunately, many attempts to isolate the VMO have it wrong and at times completely backward. If you have attempted to strengthen your VMO by squeezing something between your knees while doing squats or bridges, then that has been counterproductive. When you drive your knee inward, you strengthen a knee valgus pattern (knocked-knees). When your knee goes inward, the patella does not track properly. Rather, a healthy VMO is happiest when it gets to work with the hip abductors. So if you want to enhance any squats, wall sits, or bridges you do, place a theraband around your knees tight enough that you have to actively keep your knees neutral. This will strengthen the pattern that's needed to keep your patella tracking properly.

The quickest and simplest ways to address anterior knee and patellofemoral issues is to perform a quad stretch using a chair or stairs, followed by wide split squats and twisty superman squats.

Chair quad stretch: Using a chair or similar, rest your knee on the seat with your foot on the backrest. Drive your hips forward to stretch the quad muscles. Once a stretch is felt, gently pulse forward/backward, 20-30x.

Wide split squats: In lunge position, widen your feet approximately shoulder width. Squat straight down and up 15x, being careful to keep hips facing forward and not allowing knees to dip inward.

Twisty superman squats: Balance on one leg and reach forward with hands and upper body. Next, rotate your hips and upper body upward, allow rear leg to counterbalance your upper body. In this position, perform single-leg squat 10-15x, paying careful attention to keeping hips rotated upward and not allowing your knee to dip inward.

This area is one where you may have to look above and below to sort it out. The happiness of the patellofemoral joint is largely dependent on the ankle, knee, and hip all being on the same page and muscles firing properly. Because of this, there is a good chance you will need to look at any misbehavings of everything beneath your belly button. How do you know where to start? Consider where the biggest area of weakness is likely to be. If you have had ankle issues in the past, start there. If you think your hips might need a level-up, start there.

Medial Knee: Do Not Let Excessive Torque Happen Here

The structures around the inside of the knee that get cranky are usually the medial collateral ligament (MCL) as well as the pes anserine bursa. The tendons of your sartorius, gracilis, and semitendinosus (it's safe to Google these!) all converge at a point just below your medial knee. At this point, there is a large bursa which prevents friction between these tendons and the bone underneath. The convergence of the tendons has the appearance of a bird's foot, which is where the name "pes anserine" comes from. I hope you can use that during the next game of trivia you find yourself in!

Pain in your medial knee can be caused by a twisting mechanism, but it can also be progressive in buildup. Typically, weakness of the hip abductors, external rotators, and VMO cause the knee to fall inwards (valgus) and undergo increased rotational stress, which places more strain on the MCL and pes anserine tendons. Over time the MCL and bursa can become inflamed and sharp pain can result.

Your best bet for medial knee issues is to fix the imbalances in your hip and quads, as this should keep your knee more stable. Certainly include wide split squats as well as balancing on one leg while twisting your hips.

Wide split squats: In lunge position, widen your feet approximately shoulder width. Squat straight down and up 15x, being careful to keep hips facing forward and not allowing knees to dip inward.

Single-leg balance with hip twists: Stand on one leg as tall as you can. Staying tall, slowly pivot your hips side to side, 15x each direction, and paying careful attention not to let your hips drop.

In some people, poor forefoot stability can also contribute to medial knee pain. As you land and your body weight transfers onto your forefoot, your *peroneal muscles* (outside of lower leg) and forefoot muscles should stabilize your big toe, so you can push off. If there is weakness in the peroneals or forefoot, and the big toe is not able to have a stable base to push from, then the foot will continue pronating until it can find something stable. This extra split second of late stage *pronation* can be enough to drive the foot, and consequently the knee inward. This could be the underlying cause of your medial knee pain.

If you suspect that the foot is involved, then utilize the suggestions listed in the medial and lateral ankle sections. In other situations, limited extension of the big toe is present, causing inability to push off properly. The result is a turned-out foot and excessive stress on the medial knee. If you suspect you fall into this camp, consult the foot and plantar fascia section.

Hamstrings: If I Can Touch My Toes I'm Fine, Right?

Hamstring issues can be tricky at times. There are three hamstring muscles that originate off your ischial tuberosity (sit bone). Two extend down to your medial knee, the other extends laterally to the head of your fibula at the outside of your knee. The lateral hamstring also has a second origin point in the back of the femur. Because the hamstrings cross both the hips and knees, they are considered "two-joint muscles." This means that they affect the knees and hips at the same time. Any disconnect between the movement of the hips and knees will cause a lot of stress on the hamstrings!

Hamstring crankiness can come in many flavors, including pain in the sit bone, general tightness in the whole muscle, and sharp pain in the insertion points of each tendon. Quite often the hamstrings are flat out tight. Blame it on sitting too much or genetics, but regardless, many of us would benefit from stretching more thoroughly. Some may say they stretch regularly, but here is the tricky part: most hamstring stretches are done incorrectly. Also, in order to truly create a change in the length of the muscle, you need to hold a static stretch for up to 3-5 minutes. Many of us "stretch" by touching our toes for a few seconds then wonder why our hamstrings persist in being tight.

The main bad habit many fall into when stretching hamstrings is flexing too much from the low back rather than the hips. Picture your running buddy doing a hamstring stretch by standing and reaching toward his toes. Where does a lot of his reach come from? Quite often it comes from flexing his low back. This can create too much motion in his low back and contribute to a bad habit. Rather, he should start any hamstring stretch by arching his back before bending forward, keeping careful attention on pivoting at his hips. Males tend to be bad about this and allow bad habits to persist, which is one of the reasons we tend to have low back issues—but I digress.

Because your hamstrings are two-joint muscles, they have a lot of responsibility when it comes to running. Hamstrings do not just simply bend the knee, rather they stabilize the knee when the foot is planted and help keep your hip and core in proper alignment to push off correctly. When the knee and hip are in motion at the same time, the hamstrings get pulled in different directions. Again, when they are coordinated well, life is good. If the hip is imbalanced or the knee is unstable, then the hamstrings can get mixed signals. When the knee and hip do not agree, a tug-of-war match can ensue. How would you feel being caught in that mix?

Much of the time, tightness in the hamstrings results from weakness or confusion of the muscle. Think about it this way: as a muscle lengthens, the strength and stability decreases. A muscle is happiest when it can safely lengthen and bring itself back. Quite often the hamstring is not happy about how much pull it is getting from both ends. Because of this, it will tighten as a self-preservation technique. When it is pulled from both ends too quickly—more quickly than it can respond to—a strain occurs. A strain can be either microscopic or the other end of the spectrum which is a full rupture.

Hip imbalance is one of the biggest risk factors for hamstring injuries. Many times tightness in the hip flexors, especially the rectus femoris (quad, hip flexor, and also a two-joint muscle!), will increase the stress on the hamstrings. Mainly this occurs because of resulting glute inhibition, poor positioning of the knee, or a combination of factors.

Sorting out hamstring issues can be very tricky. It is best to discern what the underlying cause is for you. Are you prone to tightness in general? Perhaps try diligently stretching every day for several weeks and see if that makes a change. Are you suspicious that hip imbalance may be contributing? Then work on flexibility of the antagonists to the hamstrings (quads and hip flexors), as well as building up strength in the glutes and hamstrings. Is it tightness due to muscles not feeling strong in lengthened positions? The key here is to practice safely performing exercises that test stability in lengthened ranges. Single-leg deadlifts are helpful for this issue.

Hamstring stretch: Prop one foot on a chair with knee slightly bent. Arch your low back, then gently pivot forward at your hips until a stretch is felt in the back of the thigh. Gently pulse hips forward and backward, 20-30x.

Single-leg deadlifts: Balance on one leg, then lean forward with your upper body, reaching straight forward. At the same time, raise the rear leg up attempting to get parallel to the ground, 10-15x on each leg.

HAMSTRINGS

If the issue is near the sit bone, it may be an inflamed structure that will not appreciate being stretched, so do not assume that a tight muscle wants to be stretched! Rather, icing, rest, and progressive strengthening may be the key. Getting to the underlying imbalance will also be critical.

Another underlying factor for this area is poor sacroiliac motion, causing increased stress on a huge ligament called the sacrotuberous ligament. This ligament attaches your sacrum to the ischial tuberosity. Because of their common attachment and sharing of fibers, when this ligament becomes inflamed, it can also cause inflammation at the origin point of the hamstrings.

If the issue is in the middle of the muscle somewhere, there is a good chance stretching will be helpful. There is also a very good chance that a strain has occurred that will respond well to deep tissue massage—in which case, find someone with sharp elbows or a sadistic streak to help you out!

If the pain is in the hamstring tendons around your knee, then stretches will likely be helpful, but be careful to keep a slight bend in your knee when stretching. Also, look for hip imbalances and ankle restrictions, which we will cover in upcoming sections. Icing the painful area and balance/stability exercises will also be critical for this area.

Calf: Do I Just Need to Stretch More?

The calf complex is made up mostly of the gastrocnemius (higher, more prominent, two-headed) and soleus (deeper, lower) muscles. Deep to the soleus there are several long, skinny muscles that sometimes come into play with calf pain. The calf muscles have two main purposes in running: provide stability during loading and push off at the end of contact. Most of the time when the calf becomes cranky, it happens during the loading phase.

Every time your foot hits the ground, your calf is the first big muscle group that has to control the load. The first thing to consider if you are having calf pain is whether or not you have adequate flexibility. How do you know if you have adequate flexibility? Depends largely on the individual. Generally speaking, if you can drive your knee forward and touch a wall, with your foot firmly planted four to five inches away from the wall, then you are probably in good shape. If your ankle falls inward, chances are good that your body has found a faulty movement pattern to get around tightness in the calf (or an ankle restriction—check the ankle sections for more on this one!). With calf issues, thorough stretching is likely the first place to start.

Even though we think of the calf muscles as being mostly sagittal plane muscles (forward/backward), we cannot ignore the role they play with rotation as well. You need to consider this with any calf exercise you do, stretching or strengthening. A typical calf stretch is a good place to start, but putting a rotational element into the stretch will make it that much more thorough.

Calf stretch: Lean against a wall or similar with one leg extended behind you. Gently drive forward 30x with your hips to stretch your calf muscles, keeping your heel on the ground.

Twisty calf stretch: In the calf stretch position, lean forward with your hips until a stretch is felt. Next, rotate your hips right and left, allowing your knee and ankle to rotate as well, 30x.

Sometimes the calf muscles are simply not strong enough to withstand the pounding you place on them with every step. The calf muscles need to lengthen during loading before they push off. This creates an eccentric contraction of the calves. If the strength of the muscles fail or begin to fatigue, then the muscles will either tighten up as a defense mechanism, or become strained. Typically it will tighten up after the strain occurs as well, since the muscle will not want to be lengthened under load that deeply.

If strength is the underlying issue, then begin with simple calf raises off a step. As that becomes easier, progress into doing these with one leg at a time and adding a twist by starting with your foot turned in and out.

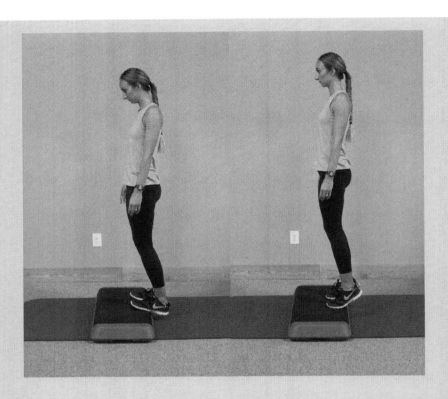

Calf raises: Stand on the edge of a step. Rise up onto your toes and slowly lower down so your heels are below the height of the step, 30x.

Single-leg calf raises: Stand on one leg on the edge of a step. Rise up onto your toes and slowly lower down so your heel is below the height of the step, 15-30x.

Inverted calf raise: Perform single-leg calf raise with your foot turned inward, 15-30x.

Everted calf raise: Perform single-leg calf raise with your foot turned outward, 15-30x.

If you have undergone any level of strain, it would be characterized by consistently sharp pain in the same spot. Quite often, strain will result in localized tightness around the sharp area. Stretching for this is one element, but often more direct myofascial work is helpful. A foam roller or ball can be helpful but may not be specific or aggressive enough. Similar to hamstring injuries, your best bet is often to have a friend, teammate, or therapist get their hands on you. Once the strained area is loosened up, then regular stretching and strengthening will be more effective.

Imbalances higher up the leg can also be a major contributor to calf issues. Any weakness in your core, glutes, quads, or hamstrings will place more load on the calves. Think of your calves as being the first muscle to respond, but also the last line of defense when it comes to keeping your face off the ground. The loading process should be a team effort between all the muscles from your core down. Since the calf muscles are the closest to the ground, they can often become the most picked on. Anytime your calves are becoming unhappy, take a glance at any potential misbehavings higher up and this will give you a clue why.

Calf issues can also be complicated. Old ankle injuries and foot issues can be huge underlying factors. We will cover these in greater detail in the coming sections. But please consider that your simple calf issue may have some tricky underlying factors. For instance, an old ankle sprain may have left your fibula bone slightly unstable. Your soleus, tibialis posterior, and flexor hallucis longus originate partially from the fibula. If your fibula bone is not where it is supposed to be, when it is supposed to be there, the muscles will not be happy about it. These muscles will tend to tighten up and/or become strained due to being pulled in the wrong directions.

The bones of your foot can also fall out of alignment or lack proper mobility. When this happens, foot issues often occur, but the calf can also take the brunt. If stretching and strengthening do not seem to be getting you anywhere, then consider what else is contributing to the crankiness.

Another underlying factor for calf crankiness has to do with your foot placement at the moment of impact. Many people have opted to land with their toes or forefoot hitting first. This is also known as a forefoot strike pattern. I will avoid a long dissertation on whether this is a good idea or not at this point. But it is important to understand that a forefoot strike pattern will automatically transfer more load to the calves away from the higher muscles. For some people, this may be a positive thing. For others it may be detrimental. Please do not just assume that it is the best for everyone. Each person has his or her own needs and shortcomings. If you run with a forefoot strike pattern, this could be your underlying factor for calf pain.

Medial Shin: The Dreaded Shin Splints

Medial shin pain is characterized by often sharp and intense pain along the inside part of the tibia bone. The causes and onset can be complicated and garner fancy names (e.g., medial tibial stress syndrome, tibialis posterior tendinitis, stress fractures or reactions, *compartment syndrome*). Several structures come into play: the tibia bone itself, the surrounding fascia and connective tissue, and the muscles. There are three long, skinny muscles that originate deep in your calf before surfacing along the medial shin. You have likely heard of the tibialis posterior, with the flexor digitorum longus and flexor hallucis longus being the lesser known partners in crime. Quite often one of these muscles becomes cranky and is the source of pain.

The tibialis posterior inserts onto the underside of the bones of your midfoot. The primary objective of this muscle is to keep your arch supported. Every time your foot hits the ground, you will pronate. Pronation (foot flattening inward) is a good thing as it is part of the overall biomechanical loading process, however too much pronation is not a good thing. As your foot lands and the arch begins to flatten, your tibialis posterior lengthens. As you begin the transition from full loading to pushing off, the tibialis posterior will try to shorten to help restore the arch. When your foot gracefully supinates and pushes off, then life is good. If your foot does not quickly restore itself, then watch out!

The flexor digitorum longus (FDL) and flexor hallucis longus (FHL) muscles also start deep in the calf, with the tendons of these muscles running just behind the medial ankle bone before extending all the way to the tips of your toes. The FHL attaches onto the big toe, the FDL the other four. These muscles are not often blamed for medial shin pain, but they can still be a factor. Specifically, any limitation in these muscles will affect how well your toes can extend. Lack of extension in your toes will be most critical as you push off. Poor push off can cause your foot to twist or contort in an awkward way and contribute to increased burden on the calf, tibialis posterior, or the joints of your foot and ankle.

The tibia bone itself warrants attention here as well. During the normal loading-unloading process, the tibia bone goes through a slight corkscrew motion. As your right foot lands and pronates, the tibia will rotate counterclockwise. Once the transition from full loading to pushing off occurs, the tibia will rotate clockwise as the foot supinates. Sounds great, right? What could possibly go wrong with this picture? Unfortunately a lot can go wrong here. If the tibia rotates too far, or does not rotate enough, shin pain can be the result. This can make the process of resolving pain rather tricky.

When the tibia rotates too far, the three muscles we covered already will become overburdened, especially the tibialis posterior. The origin point of the muscle is the back of the tibia bone. Quite often this is where the pain originates due to the muscle tugging too much on the bone.

When the tibia does not rotate enough (due to tight calf or ankle restrictions), then the tibia bone itself is left in a precarious position where the shock of landing travels right through the bone instead of being absorbed by the muscles. Picture jumping up as high as you can, then landing with your knees locked. Pretty painful, right? The jolt of landing with your joints locked places a lot of stress on the bones, ligaments, and joint surfaces. Of course we would rather land with knees bent, which allows the muscles to absorb the shock.

In the same way, a tibia bone that rotates appropriately will allow for the muscles to absorb the shock. A tibia bone that stays rigid will take too much of the shock. Over time, the bone itself will respond unhappily by either developing a stress fracture/reaction, or the surrounding soft tissues (aka periosteum) will become inflamed and thickened.

Other factors that can cause increased stress on the medial tibia include weakness in the glutes, as well as weakness in the forefoot. In short, weakness in the glutes or other hip imbalances can cause too much ground contact time due to poor load management. Increased ground contact time means that the foot will stay in the deeply pronated position for a few hundredths of a second longer than is ideal. Multiply that by thousands of steps and you have the makings of cranky muscles.

Weakness or poor joint mobility of the forefoot can also contribute to medial shin issues. Every time you push off, you need enough stability from your forefoot and specifically your big toe. The big toe becomes ready to push off when the muscles and joints have been loaded properly. Any weakness in the muscles that influence the big toe (peroneals, flexor hallucis longus and brevis) will cause the foot to go deeper into a pronated position. The joints of the big toe and forefoot can also become restricted. Sometimes it is acquired, sometimes it is congenital. Either way, if this is a factor for you, it is important to work on the clean motion of your foot to allow for proper joint mechanics.

Feeling overwhelmed with the intricacies of the medial shin? Again, it can be tricky and often is not even the shin's fault. Certainly take the time to discern if any hip or ankle issues are contributing. The first exercises to perform every day are calf stretches with a twist to encourage proper tibial rotation as well as calf raises off a step or curb. Once you can easily do 30 reps of a calf raise, then progress by performing them on one leg with your foot turned in and out.

Twisty calf stretch: In the calf stretch position, lean forward with your hips until a stretch is felt. Next, rotate your hips right and left, allowing your knee and ankle to rotate as well, 30x.

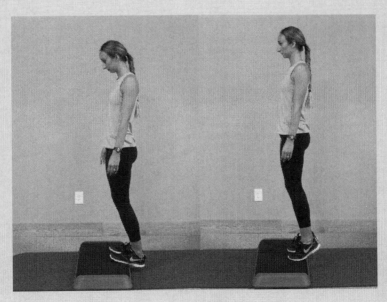

Calf raises: Stand on the edge of a step. Rise up onto your toes and slowly lower down so your heels are below the height of the step, 30x.

Inverted calf raise: Perform single-leg calf raise with your foot turned inward, 15-30x.

Everted calf raise: Perform single-leg calf raise with your foot turned outward, 15-30x.

MEDIAL SHIN

If your shins do not improve with these movements, then consider what other factors are contributing. Are your hips as strong and flexible as they should be? If not, then put in the work to address your hips and see if your shins improve. Are there issues with your form or ability to balance on one leg? If so, these could be underlying factors for too much ground contact time or landing in a poor way, putting more strain on the medial shin muscles.

In certain situations, shin and calf pain can come from more serious issues such as stress fractures and compartment syndrome, which are much more complicated to diagnose and treat. If you suspect that discomfort you are having is deeper than simple muscle crankiness, please do not hesitate to get it checked out by your trusted medical provider.

Anterior Shin: The Other Version of Shin Splints? Or Another Animal Altogether?

Pain in the anterior or front of the shin is less common than the medial shin, but no less painful and frustrating. Typically pain in this area comes from crankiness of the tibialis anterior and/or extensor hallucis longus muscles. The pain can be in the muscles themselves, or at the attachments onto the bone.

Pain in this area can often come from quadriceps tightness, especially the rectus femoris. The quads and anterior shin muscles share a lot of connective tissue attachments around the knee. Because of this, any misbehavings of either party will affect the other. Typically, tight quads causing inhibition of the anterior shin muscles is the pattern we see. When this type of imbalance is present, the shin muscles struggle to do their job appropriately during initial loading.

If you suspect that imbalance between the quads and anterior shin muscles is part of the equation, start with a quad chair stretch. Even though the shin muscles may feel tight, it is often difficult to stretch them directly. Feel free to also use a tennis ball to self-massage. After stretching your quads, perform heel-big-toe walking as a way to restore balance between the quads and anterior shin.

115

Chair quad stretch: Using a chair or similar, rest your knee on the seat with your foot on the backrest. Drive your hips forward to stretch the quad muscles. Once a stretch is felt, gently pulse forward/backward, 20-30x.

Heel big toe walking: Raise your lateral toes off the ground. Slowly walk forward and backward keeping lateral toes off the ground and weight on your heels and big toes, 30-60 seconds.

Another factor that can contribute to anterior shin pain is bony misalignment and mobility restrictions of the ankle. It is very common for the joints of the ankle to become stiff in some directions, and/or unstable in other directions. Ankle sprains are especially notorious for leaving residual effects months or years down the road. Since the tendons of the anterior shin muscles travel across the ankle bones, they can easily become irritated when the bones are not moving as they should. An irritated tendon will cause the muscle to tighten up as a protective mechanism. If you suspect that ankle issues are an underlying factor, then check out the section for suggestions on dealing with anterior and lateral ankle issues.

Medial Ankle: It Must Be Because I'm a Pronator

Pain in the medial or inner ankle usually comes from inflammation of the soft tissues that surround the tendons of the three medial shin muscles (tibialis posterior, flexor digitorum longus, and flexor hallucis longus). These tendons run behind the medial ankle bone (medial malleolus) which acts as a pulley for the tendons. Friction can build up in this area very easily which will inflame the synovial sheath around the tendons.

Bear with me for a quick geek-out moment. The tendons themselves do not get inflamed. Each tendon has connective tissue around it, including a sheath that holds cushioning fluid called synovial fluid. When there is too much friction, the sheath will swell up and become very tender. For many years this has been labeled as "tendinitis." Tendinitis is technically impossible, since the inflammation is not **within** the tendon. However, the inflammation will be in the peripheral structures **around** the tendon, so in many ways the treatment does not change even if it is not called by the correct name. Many have voiced that "tendinitis" does not exist, and have unfortunately led people to believe that we have been doing things all wrong by using ice, compression, anti-inflammatories, etc. Still, because the term "tendinitis" is so widely used and accepted in the medical community and society as a whole, please do not get hung up on the terminology. Again, the term tendinitis is incorrect, but if anyone is making a big deal out of it, they are likely trying to pick an argument.

I'll climb down from the soapbox now. Many now use the term "tendinopathy" instead, which is more general, but certainly not inaccurate. Regardless, if it hurts, then something is wrong. If there is pain behind and just below the medial ankle, there's a good chance that the tendons and supporting structures are not happy. As discussed in the medial shin section, any imbalance or weakness that causes increased stress on the three muscles can manifest itself with pain in the muscles or tendons. The underlying biomechanical causes can be the same for shin pain as ankle pain so rather than reiterate it again here, please check out that section.

Poor stability or mobility of the ankle and midfoot can also be a cause of medial ankle pain. The talus (primary ankle bone) rests on the calcaneus (heel bone) and navicular (just in front of the ankle). Every time your foot hits the ground, the calcaneus rotates, driving the talus medially. This also drives the tibial rotation that we covered in the medial shin section. If there is excessive mobility of the talus inward, this will cause increased stress on the three tendons, as well as the deltoid ligament and spring ligament (aka calcaneonavicular ligament), which support the medial ankle. Look up pictures of these ligaments, then imagine for yourself what it would feel like to have them overstretched a few thousand times. Could that be where your medial ankle pain is coming from?

MEDIAL ANKLE

If you suspect that increased stress of the medial ankle is part of the equation for you, practice balancing on one leg while kicking your other foot across your body. Also, this may require hands-on help to ensure the talus bone is not stuck and able to move laterally, as this will drive it too far medial. Ankle mobilizations may also be helpful, being very careful not to instigate further pain.

Ankle mobilization with inversion: Stand with the targeted ankle behind the other and turn your foot inward. In this position, gently drive your knee forward keeping your heel on the ground, 20-30x. You may wish to lean against a wall for balance.

*Single-leg balance with reach across: Balance on one leg.
Reach across your body with your other foot and lightly tap
the floor as far away from your body as you can reach
at a 45-degree angle, 15-20x.*

It is worth mentioning again that any general weakness of your foot, calf, or hips can contribute to the ankle being overburdened. With many of the areas mentioned, if you are able to gain strength, it will enhance your ability to land and push off more quickly and efficiently. The medial ankle structures will certainly thank you for any help they get to unload more quickly!

Anterior and Lateral Ankle: My Ankle Sprain from Five Years Ago?

The anterior and lateral ankle area can also be tricky to progress. The majority of painful issues in this area result from previous injuries, even ones from many years ago. Following an ankle sprain, it is very common for the bones to be out of alignment, which affects their ability to move properly while walking and running. With every step, the tibia, talus, and fibula should move in a coordinated dance to allow for loading and unloading. In order to do this appropriately, the bones have to start in their proper place, be guided by healthy muscles, tendons, and ligaments, and then return to their proper place. When you injure your ankle, it is more common than not that this process will be disrupted.

In the acute phase, right after an ankle roll/sprain, inflammation and stiffness is usually present. Inflammation initially comes from the ligaments being stretched or torn. At this point, many people assume that a few days or weeks of "taking it easy" will heal everything properly. Unfortunately, this is usually not the case. The initial inflammation will work itself out, but you are often left with bones that have shifted which inhibits the full healing of the ligaments, tendons, and joint surfaces.

What you are left with is joints that are bonking into each other instead of dancing gracefully. You are also left with inhibition of the surrounding muscles since the muscles take their cues from the tendons and ligaments. The pain can come from any combination of the joint surfaces (between the talus, tibia, fibula, calcaneus, and midfoot bones) from direct impact or rubbing friction. The pain can also come from an injured ligament that has not healed properly and is constantly being overstretched. Since ligaments hold bones together, if those bones are not playing nice, the ligament is often the collateral damage.

Because of this, you need to ensure the bones are in their proper place at rest and move appropriately while you run. The talus bone is prone to rest further forward than it should. The fibula bone is prone to being stuck forward as well, both of which leave the tibia unable to rotate appropriately. The fibula bone may also be slightly separated from the tibia.

Some restrictions in the bones are able to be improved on your own. The easiest exercise to do at home is the ankle mobilization. There are other more complicated ways to self-mobilize the bones using straps and other devices. Feel free to dabble with these as well!

Ankle mobilization: Stand with the targeted ankle behind the other. In this position, gently drive your knee forward straight and slightly to the right and left, keeping your heel on the ground, 20-30x. You may wish to lean against a wall for balance.

Once the bones are in alignment and moving properly, restoring ligament and muscular stability is absolutely crucial. The place to start for this is single-leg balance exercises. Once you can stand without losing your balance, it is important to be stable while moving. Start by standing on one leg, and reach out with your toes to touch imaginary spots on the floor in the shape of a compass. As you improve, continue to challenge your balance by doing single-leg calf raises as well as spot jumps.

Compass floor touches: Balance on one leg. Reach with your other foot to lightly touch the floor in the directions of a compass, 10x each direction.

Single-leg calf raises: Stand on one leg on the edge of a step. Rise up onto your toes and slowly lower down so your heel is below the height of the step, 15-30x.

Spot jumps: Place pieces of tape on the ground or floor in the shape of a box. Balance on one leg and jump from spot to spot, 30-60 seconds each leg.

ANTERIOR AND LATERAL ANKLE

The peroneal muscles are a critical area to strengthen in order to recover from and prevent ankle sprains. These three muscles run along the outside of your lower leg and attach in the midfoot. The tendons of these muscles will often be collateral damage with ankle issues, which will inhibit the strength of the muscles themselves. These muscles are rarely strengthened properly since most approaches involve using a theraband to perform resisted ankle eversion. The best way to strengthen them is when your foot is on the ground, not hanging out in space. If you have a rocker board, perform single-leg rocks with the foot pointed slightly outward. If you do not have a rocker board, single-leg calf raises off a step with your foot turned out will also target these muscles well.

Rocker board with eversion: Balance on one leg on a rocker board with your foot turned outward approximately 20 degrees. Perform calf raises on the board, 30x.

Everted calf raise: Perform single-leg calf raise with your foot turned outward, 15-30x.

All too often, an unresolved ankle sprain will lead to another. When you have sprained your ankle multiple times, your body will often have a pretty good memory of that, and will sprain or roll more easily. This is not good! Some people have reported that it does not hurt to roll their ankle anymore. This is also not good! This indicates that their ligaments are so compromised that they provide no support for the ankle. Some may be able to run like this for a time, but it will compromise muscle balance and proper motion further up the leg. It is worthwhile to be proactive about your ankles even if you feel they are a lost cause!

Achilles Tendon: I've Been Running a Lot of Hills Lately

The Achilles tendon attaches the two main calf muscles (gastrocnemius and soleus) to the heel bone. It is a very strong structure but can easily become cranky if it is overburdened. The term "tendinitis" is often used to describe any amount of tenderness. Inflammation is what causes the tenderness, although the inflammation is not found within the tendon. Rather, there are several bursa sacs around the Achilles that are present to cushion and prevent friction between the tendon and surrounding structures. These bursa sacs will swell up when they are under too much stress.

Why do they swell up and what are the causes? That is where things can get complicated. The simplest thing that can happen is your calf being too tight. Tightness in the calf muscles, which is all too common for runners, can compress the bursa and restrict the motion of the calcaneus (heel bone). Because of this, the first thing to address to sort out Achilles pain is to regain flexibility in the calf muscles. Do this by stretching your calf with your knee straight and knee bent. If it is painful to stretch, then do not push through the pain but keep the depth of stretch within a pain-free range. Also, any foam rolling or self-massage is fair game!

Calf stretch: Lean against a wall or similar with one leg extended behind you. Gently drive forward 30x with your hips to stretch your calf muscles, keeping your heel on the ground.

Calf stretch knee bent: Lean against a wall or similar with one leg behind the other, keeping a slight bend in the rear leg. Gently drive forward 30x with your hips to stretch your lower calf muscle, keeping your heel on the ground.

Another common underlying factor is weakness of the calf muscles. When this occurs, extra tension will be placed on the Achilles due to the muscles not being able to absorb the load of each step. Often this will progress into significant muscle tightness that does not improve with stretching. So if simple stretches for several weeks are not helping you progress, spend time performing single-leg calf raises off a step to build up the strength and loading capacity.

Single-leg calf raises: Stand on one leg on the edge of a step. Rise up onto your toes and slowly lower down so your heel is below the height of the step, 15-30x.

ACHILLES TENDON

Limitations in the joint mobility of the calcaneus (heel bone) can also irritate the Achilles. Every time your foot hits the ground (regardless of heel or forefoot strike!), the calcaneus should move side to side. This is a normal part of the pronation-supination process that your foot should go through with every step. The calcaneus should move side to side like the rudder of a boat. During this brief, subtle, movement, the load is spread out through all the muscles, ligaments, and tendons that attach nearby. When the movement is restricted, the tendon is stuck in the middle to absorb all the shock. To test the motion of the calcaneus, simply grasp your heel bone and wiggle it side to side, then compare it to the other side. If you see a difference, then perform thirty self-mobilizations of the side to side movement every day until it feels equal to the other leg. You are essentially knocking the rust off a stiff joint.

Another underlying factor of Achilles issues is tightness in the hamstrings. Because of strong fascial connections, any tightness in the hamstrings is liable to cause increased tension on the Achilles and calf muscles. If you suspect this may be a factor, work hamstring stretches into your weekly routine.

Hamstring stretch: Prop one foot on a chair with knee slightly bent. Arch your low back, then gently pivot forward at your hips until a stretch is felt in the back of the thigh. Gently pulse hips forward and backward, 20-30x.

Another factor that has come into play more recently is the shoes you wear. For decades, running shoes typically had around 12 millimeters of height difference between the heel and the toe. With higher heels in shoes, the Achilles is in a shortened and more relaxed position. With the arrival of minimalist footwear, the shoe companies have adapted many of their shoes to accommodate. The result of this is that shoes can have anywhere from zero heel-toe drop up to the traditional height. Many models are in the four- to eight-millimeter range. While this factor may seem trivial, if you have run in a certain shoe for years, then switch to something with a few millimeters less, you better believe your Achilles is going to notice. Decide for yourself if the shoes you wear are contributing by running a few times in something with a higher heel height. If this decreases your pain then this is likely a factor for you. If you are in the process of intentionally transitioning into more minimalist footwear, some crankiness in the Achilles can be expected. Please be very careful about adapting your footwear in this way—allow plenty of time for your body to catch up to the new stresses placed on it.

Another potential contributor is the way your foot strikes the ground. Along with the minimalist movement, many have adapted to landing on their forefoot, instead of heel. Again, this has benefits in some ways, but also potential detriments. One of the detriments is that more work is transferred to the calf and Achilles when you use a forefoot strike. Essentially, the calf and Achilles are always under tension and stay in a shortened position, as opposed to a heel or midfoot strike where the calf and Achilles have a chance to relax and lengthen with each stride. Remember from the flexibility chapter that proper lengthening of a muscle allows you to utilize free elastic energy. When you shortcut the lengthening phase, your muscles have to work harder to generate the needed force. If your Achilles pain has come on the heels of adopting a forefoot strike pattern, consider whether that was the best move for you!

Foot and Plantar Fascia: I Just Need New Shoes, Right?

Why does foot pain come in a myriad of different forms? There are several reasons. One reason is that your foot is the contact point on the ground, which means it is ground zero for the meeting of forces between your body and the ground. Think about Physics 101; for every force, there is an equal and opposite force. Every time you strike the ground, you are delivering a force to the ground. The ground does not go anywhere, which means that the ground pushes right back on you with the same amount of force. Your foot is the first line of defense for absorbing that force so it can be properly dissipated and used to load up the next stride. Essentially, your foot is constantly colliding with an immovable object.

Because your foot is the first line of defense, any chinks in the armor will be exposed. Many times, the pain you feel is simply the weakest link in a dysfunctional movement pattern. The weakest ligament may become cranky because the nearest bones have stopped moving correctly. Similarly, the weakest muscle may be painful, even though it has not misbehaved. It is taking the brunt of another's bad habits above or below.

Quite often, the underlying factors are similar from a biomechanical standpoint. The actual site of pain however, can be much more tricky. The foot is made up of 26 different bones, with 33 unique joint movements. The joint movements of the foot are subtle, but very critical. If any of these joints begin to move improperly, the result can be pain at that spot, or pain in an adjacent spot that is now taking the brunt of the neighbor. If the pain is in a joint or ligament, it can come from lack of proper movement (hypomobility) or too much movement (hypermobility and instability).

To make the foot even more complicated, there are dozens of muscles, tendons, and ligaments crammed into a small space. Any of these are liable to misbehave and become painful, or tighten up and cause something else to be painful. For our purposes, we will only cover the most common areas—otherwise this section could be a book all by itself!

The most common malady of the foot is plantar fascia (PF) pain. You have likely heard of plantar fasciitis or fasciopathy. The plantar fascia is a tight band of connective tissue that originates off the heel bone and attaches onto the bases of the five toes. The PF is present to provide stability to the foot, essentially keeping the arch in place and anchoring the muscles that run throughout the foot. So what could possibly cause the PF to become unhappy? Unfortunately, many things can be underlying factors of PF pain.

Calf tightness can easily cause the plantar fascia to become cranky. As your calf muscle travels downward, it gradually becomes the Achilles tendon. The Achilles then attaches onto your calcaneus (heel bone), which is also where the PF originates. Around the calcaneus, the Achilles and PF actually share a lot of connective tissue fibers. Because of their common attachments, the calf/Achilles and the plantar fascia play tug-of-war with the heel bone. Most of the time the calf/Achilles wins out!

Calf tightness is a common underlying factor for many foot issues because of the effect it can have on the motion of the heel bone. With most foot issues, the first exercise to perform is a simple calf stretch with your knee straight, and your knee bent.

Calf stretch: Lean against a wall or similar with one leg extended behind you. Gently drive forward 30x with your hips to stretch your calf muscles, keeping your heel on the ground.

Calf stretch, knee bent: Lean against a wall or similar with one leg behind the other, keeping a slight bend in the rear leg. Gently drive forward 30x with your hips to stretch your lower calf muscle, keeping your heel on the ground.

Plantar fascia pain can also be the result of the bones of your foot being out of alignment. At rest, the bones should nicely fall into line to form your arch. Due to injury, weakness, or genetics, it is common for a bone to fall out of alignment. When this happens, the arch can be placed under more tension. The common bones to misbehave in this way are the talus, cuboid, navicular, and first metatarsal. If a bone is out of alignment, it is difficult to restore it on your own, but is certainly worth a try! Simply massaging the bottom of your foot and accentuating the arch is the easiest to try at home. Use either your hands or a ball. If you suspect there is a bone out of alignment or not moving properly, do not hesitate to visit your trusted medical provider as these can be difficult to diagnose and correct.

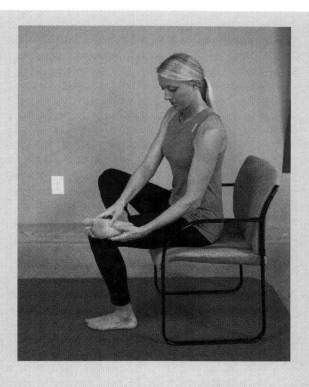

Foot self-massage: Sit with your leg propped and relaxed. Using your thumbs or knuckles, massage the muscles of your arch. Start with light pressure and progressively deepen your pressure, one to two minutes.

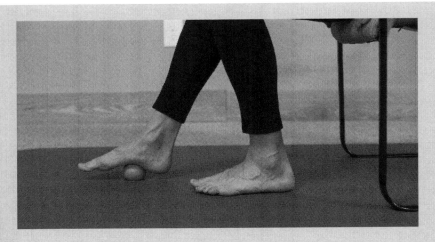

Ball arch roller: Place a tennis, lacrosse, or golf ball under the arch of your foot. Begin by gently rolling forward and backward and progressively place more weight through the foot, one to two minutes. Be careful to avoid any spot that feels bony.

Limited extension of the big toe is another common factor for plantar fascia pain and other foot issues. You need approximately 30 degrees of extension of the big toe in order to push off efficiently. If your big toe does not have enough flexibility, it forces your foot to roll to one side or the other instead of going right over top the big toe. Think about the mechanics of your foot for a moment. As you make the transition from loading your foot to pushing off, the point of biggest load shifts from the rearfoot to the forefoot. The last point of contact should come from the big toe, with a hearty propulsive force coming from the big toe. This propulsive force can only come if the big toe has been loaded properly.

The analogy I like to use is a pole vaulter. Contrast the vaulter who clears the bar with ease with one who misses off to the side. The vaulter who is successful sticks the pole and delivers a tremendous bend to the pole. This bend loads up the potential energy of the pole, which then delivers a major lift to the vaulter. A healthy big toe should behave in a similar way. A restricted big toe is more like a novice vaulter who is not able to bend the pole to create needed potential energy. When the bend is not there, the vaulter has minimal lift and usually glances off to the side.

In the same way, a restricted big toe will significantly affect your ability to push off effectively. The foot will often roll inward and create a heel whip or other visible form deviations. The unhealthy roll of the foot can also create extra pivoting in the forefoot, which will contribute to conditions such as Morton's neuroma, sesamoiditis, and metatarsalgia. Feel free to Google those terms rather than read about them in depth here! Simply put, these describe trickier types of pain around the base of your toes and forefoot.

In order to discern if limited big toe motion is a factor for you, simply sit down with your body weight forward on your forefeet. In this position, if you can pick up your big toe at least 30 degrees, then you are probably safe. If you are unable to do so, or pain is elicited while you perform this self-test, then you are likely restricted and would benefit from improved flexibility. In order to improve your big toe extension, perform a calf stretch with your big toe propped on a towel.

Big toe extension self-test: Sit with your knees overtop your toes. Raise your big toe upward (left). If you cannot raise upward at least 30 degrees (right), then tightness in this area is likely a contributing factor for you. Refer back to this test when needed to gauge progress.

Calf stretch with big toe extension: Prop your big toe on an object to elevate it. Step forward with your other foot and perform a calf stretch by gently rocking hips forward, 30x. Stretch should be felt in the calf and arch of your foot.

Another stealthy underlying factor for foot issues is intrinsic weakness of the foot itself. Many times, distance runners have not developed proper intrinsic strength and dexterity of their feet. Compared to team sport athletes who rely on more agile movements, runners' feet tend to be more one-dimensional. This comes into play as the little muscles that stabilize and fine tune the movement of the feet are unable to do their job during the thousands of landings incurred while running.

In order to develop better strength and stability of the feet, (which all runners need!) a great exercise to start with is to simply balance on one leg. Then progress to small jumps on one leg, and ultimately spot jumps for dynamic control.

Single-leg balance: Balance on one leg keeping your hips elevated, 30-60 seconds.

Spot jumps: Place pieces of tape on the ground or floor in the shape of a box. Balance on one leg and jump from spot to spot, 30-60 seconds each leg.

In order to develop better dexterity, alternating toe lifts are the first exercise to practice. Many runners struggle at first with this one, but as you get better at it, try performing the toe lifts while balancing on one leg.

Alternating toe lifts: Raise your big toe up as high as you can while pressing the other four toes firmly into the ground. Next, press your big toe firmly into the ground while raising the other four. Repeat 30x. Perform on one leg to challenge yourself further.

Not sure whether your feet are strong enough? A simple test for foot strength is to run as high up on your toes as you can. If your overall form turns wobbly, then foot weakness is a factor for you. In this situation, I recommend running on your toes for 30 second stints as part of your warm-up and sprinkled into your easy runs as well.

Conclusion

This book is all about you. The goal is to help YOU figure out what exercises will keep you running efficiently and pain-free. This book is not about "what the latest research shows." Indeed, scientific research is important and provides the needed framework for medical practice. But at the end of the day, it is all about you and what works for your story.

In my day-to-day interactions with patients and clients, I have found it critical to test each potential exercise and see how the individual responds. This, to me, is more valuable than following a formulaic protocol. The same goes for you. The descriptions and recommendations in this book could easily be seen as formulaic, but my hope is that they will be treated as lines of defense.

If you are struggling with shin issues, the first exercises to try are the ones listed in the shin sections. If they are not making a difference, then consider whether the pain you are feeling is at the root of the issue. Perhaps you have weak and tight calves without knowing it. If the shin exercises are not working, try the calf exercises and see if they have effect on your shins. Perhaps you have weakness in your hips that has never resulted in pain because your body is good at compensating.

This definitely puts more responsibility on you, but it also allows you to be more empowered and in control of your body. Would you rather be dependent on someone else, or able to take care of your own body?

If you are not sure where to start, my recommendation is to go through the whole list of exercises and pick one or two that seem the most relevant for you. For the next week, add that exercise or two into your warm-up routine and see how you feel on those runs. Even a glimmer of progress can be a positive sign that you are doing the correct thing that needs further reinforcement.

Let us revisit our hypothetical runners from the introduction. The first place Molly should start is with the exercises suggested in the medial shin section. Ideally, she should begin those at least six weeks prior to her season beginning. She begins doing the suggested exercises but does not seem to notice much change. So, like a good scientist, she begins her case study of one. She has always been accused of walking like a duck, so her first thought is that perhaps weakness in her hips is contributing. She commits to the exercises suggested for lateral hip deficiencies for two weeks. At the end of the two weeks, she notices that her running feels smoother and she is not pounding as hard.

CONCLUSION

Also, her shins have felt much better. With these indicators, Molly realizes that her hips need to get stronger. Armed with this knowledge, she is able to prepare for her upcoming season and subsequent seasons with greater confidence, and she finally reaches the podium at the state finals.

Dave has also become fed up with his hamstrings. He commits to stretching his hamstrings and notices a little progress, but still feels limited. Upon reflection, he has always felt like his hips and knees are stiff, regardless of his running. Because of this, he decides to give other hip and knee stretches a chance. He performs the chair quad stretch before his next run and immediately feels that his stride is more open and his hamstrings seem more relaxed. He is also landing softer and with his feet underneath him. He was previously prone to over-striding. His hamstrings fall back into their old habits after five miles, but Dave has seen the light and commits to stretching his quads and hip flexors regularly. With this in his warm-up and maintenance routines, he is able to stay healthy during peak mileage and crushes a few hill workouts. These would have previously resulted in needing a week off. With his greater consistency, Dave approaches his upcoming marathon feeling prepared and confident, and finally hits his Boston qualifying time.

Your story may not have a clean sitcom plot line like Molly and Dave, but it is still your story and the ending is up to you! It is worth it to take the time in experimenting to see what your body responds best to. Again, the suggested exercises for each body part are the best places to start, but do not hesitate to venture into the surrounding areas if you suspect the misbehaving area is not where the pain is.

Your body constantly needs tuning and sharpening. No one else can do that for you. May this book serve you well as you strive for your goals. Run fast, friend!

Glossary of Terms

Compartment syndrome: A condition, usually in the lower leg, that occurs when the fascia, (connective tissue) swells up between the muscles, causing pain directly as well as restriction of blood flow.

Dynamic stretching: Stretching with movement. The goal of dynamic stretching is to wake up the neuromuscular movement patterns and develop proper patterns. Done properly, this will work against the development of imbalances and loosen up joint capsules.

FABER test: FABER stands for flexion, abduction, and external rotation; the test is used to evaluate hip, lumbar spine, or SI joint restrictions.

Fascia: The network of connective tissue fibers that runs all over your body. Physiologically, they are like thousands of little elastic fibers that adapt to the movement patterns your muscles develop. Within the fascia, energy can be stored and unloaded with each stride when it behaves properly. Fascia can also be tight in an area of injury or misbehaving muscle. Fascial restrictions respond best to massage and sustained total body stretches like yoga positions.

Glutes: Often referred to collectively. Your glutes are comprised of the maximus, medius, and minimus. The glute med and min mostly work together and have tendencies toward weakness and tightness. They are deep and more lateral, relative to the glute max. The glute max is bigger, more posterior and superficial compared to the min and med. The glute max is a powerful hip rotator, as well as extensor for landing and pushing off efficiently.

Hip abductors: Group of three muscles on the outside of your hip—the glutes min and med and tensor fascia latae (TFL). These muscles often become weak and imbalanced, which translates to poor hip stability while running. This lack of hip stability can be an underlying factor for hip, low back, knee, shin, and foot issues.

Hip external rotators: Group of muscles on the back of your hip. The glute max and piriformis are the most commonly referred to external rotators. Rotation of the hip is not usually considered while running, as our hip swings forward and backward. Strength is needed with these muscles in order to absorb the landing force with each stride.

Hip flexors: A group of six muscles in the front of each hip, comprised of the psoas, iliacus, rectus femoris, tensor fascia latae, sartorius, and pectineus. Together they raise the hip upward, but subtle imbalances can occur between these muscles as well.

GLOSSARY OF TERMS

Joint capsules: A strong group of ligaments that hold each joint together deep to the muscles. Oftentimes, the joint capsules are more in need of loosening up than the muscles themselves to allow for full range of motion. Dynamic stretching done properly will successfully loosen up the joint capsules as you prepare to run. Many of the nerve endings responsible for proprioception are found in the joint capsules. Thus, properly behaving joints will directly help muscles to fire efficiently.

Joint misalignment: Any situation in which two adjacent bones are not lined up properly. This is very common in the SI joints, pelvis, ankle, and foot.

Muscle imbalance: When two or more muscles are not working well together. Every step you take requires the precise coordination of dozens of muscles. Very often, a muscle will misbehave by either firing too much, too quickly, or not enough. In any of these circumstances, the other muscles will have to change how they work. If this happens often enough, your body begins to think of it as "normal." Imbalances and compensations left unchecked will lead to injuries over time.

Neuromuscular: Refers to the interaction of the muscles and nerves. The muscles fire when the nerves tell them to. The coordination of the muscles is critical to running efficiently.

Peroneal muscles: Three long skinny muscles on the outside of your lower leg, also known as the ankle evertors. Often these muscles are strengthened incorrectly. The most important thing these muscles do is stabilize your forefoot, especially the big toe.

Pronation: The subtle rolling inward of your foot and arch with each step. Pronation is a normal and healthy part of your foot biomechanics. The term has been misused in the past and often carries a negative connotation. Too much pronation is not a good thing as it can lead to foot, ankle, and shin issues. Not enough pronation can also lead to poor movement patterns and forces not able to be properly absorbed.

Proprioception: Your body's awareness of itself. A collection of subconscious neuromuscular signals that are responsible for determining when and how each muscle needs to respond.

Sacroiliac joint: Large multi-faceted joint that connects your sacrum (tailbone) to the rest of your pelvic girdle. Small subtle movements should take place in the SI joint, but it is prone to "lock up" or lack proper motion. When this occurs, other joints and muscles are affected.

Static stretching: Stretching by holding a deep stretch for an extended length of time. The goal of static stretching is to physiologically change the length of a muscle. Rarely is this type of stretching appropriate as part of your warm-up, as it can inhibit a muscle, causing it to weaken for a time.

Acknowledgments

To all the runners and coaches who have looked to me to get results, your trust means more than you know.

To my lovely and dedicated wife, thank you for your support and encouragement in seeing this book through to completion.

To my children, may you learn from my successes and failures. May you find your own way to serve others well.

Thank you to my colleagues and those I look up to in the running world, your dedication to our profession and willingness to put your ideas out there are an inspiration!

Thank you to Jennifer and Maryanna at Aloha Publishing. Your caring and professional guidance has made this project infinitely better.

Thank you to Rachel and the design team at Fusion Creative Works. You ladies rock!

About the Author

Mike Swinger is a physical therapist in beautiful Leelanau County, Michigan. He has worked closely with runners of all ages and abilities, ranging from first-time 5K runners to collegiate All-Americans, Boston qualifiers, and Ironman competitors. Sessions with Mike consist of thorough and specific manual treatments, coupled with exercises that address individual needs for flexibility, movement pattern retraining, and strengthening.

He is a frequent speaker for track and cross-country teams, where he has performed hundreds of screenings on young runners needing direction. There are many coaches who keep him on speed dial!

Mike has gained expertise in looking for the root of the issue, rather than simply appeasing the painful area. He excels at considering the whole body in determining where the dysfunction is coming from. He also enjoys observing other runners in their natural habitat and speculating where their areas of weakness are.

Mike and his wife, Sarah, have five delightful and active children. Needless to say, much of the family training is in the form of chasing around little ones! Mike and Sarah enjoy competing in running events and triathlons and look forward to the days when their children can keep up and surpass them on the roads and trails.

Connect

Subscribe to the blog at Runphys.com/blog.

Interested in having Mike speak to your team or running group? Check out the Team Consulting page at Runphys.com.

Interested in personal coaching for your next big race or to prepare for your upcoming season? Check out the Individual Coaching page at Runphys.com.

Have questions or feedback for *Runner's Fix*? Mike would love to hear from you. Email him at info@runphys.com.

Social Media:
- @mikerunphys
- @mikerunphys
- @runphys

31173248R00091